MW00567267

The Gifts of God

Helen Schucman

FOUNDATION FOR INNER PEACE

Designed by Mary Russel, Sausalito
Calligraphy by Patti Cummins, Larkspur
Composed in Bembo type by Mackenzie-Harris, San Francisco

First Printing, February, 1982
Second Printing, September, 1988

Library of Congress Catalog Card Number: 81-70309

For information contact the publisher:
Foundation for Inner Peace
Box 635
Tiburon, CA 94920

Into Christ's Presence will we enter now, serenely unaware of everything except His shining face and perfect Love. The vision of His face will stay with you, but there will be an instant which transcends all vision, even this, the holiest. This you will never teach, for you attained it not through learning. Yet the vision speaks of your remembrance of what you knew that instant, and will surely know again.

A Course In Miracles.

Contents

The Gifts of God

Introduction

BORN IN New York City on July 14, 1909, Helen Schucman had an insular and sheltered childhood. Her upper middle class parents maintained a typically Victorian household in which Helen's closest emotional relationships were with the servants who took care of her. She scarcely knew her only sibling, a brother, who was fourteen years her senior.

Helen had an eclectic religious upbringing. Although both her parents were nominally Jewish, her father ignored religion while her mother dabbled in various Protestant denominations. Neither of them was concerned with Helen's religious training. A Catholic governess and later a Baptist maid exposed her to their beliefs, which she became enthused about for a while. However, during her teens she fluctuated between atheism and agnosticism.

While attending New York University, Helen pursued her interests in literature, music and languages, and at the end of her senior year married Louis Schucman, a fellow student. At various times Helen worked briefly in her husband's bookstore, but generally found her life unfulfilling and without focus. In her forties she returned to NYU to study psychology, received her Ph.D. in 1957, and held positions as an associate research scientist and instructor. In 1958 she accepted a position at Columbia Presbyterian Medical Center where she later became Chief Psychologist at the Neurological Institute.

Helen also held an appointment as Associate Professor of Psychology in the Department of Psychiatry, College of Physicians and Surgeons, Columbia University. Until her retirement in 1976, she taught, did research, supervised clinical work and collaborated on the writing of articles and chapters for scholarly journals and books.

Throughout her career Helen emphasized the strict disciplines of research and scholarship, and had little tolerance for such "soft" interests as spirituality. However, in 1965 her department head and friend, Dr. William N. Thetford, unexpectedly announced to her that he was fed up with the competition, aggression and anger which permeated their professional lives and extended into their attitudes and relationships. He concluded that there must be another way of living —in harmony rather than discord—and he was determined to find it. To their mutual amazement, Helen enthusiastically volunteered to join him in a collaborative search. They were hardly prepared for what followed over the next ten years. Their joining served as a trigger for Helen to "hear an inner Voice dictate" an answer to their search for a better way. It came in the form of a 1,200-page self-study course in spiritual development which was published anonymously in three volumes as A COURSE IN MIRACLES.*

As Helen later described the experience:

The Voice made no sound, but seemed to be giving me a kind of rapid, inner dictation which I took down in a shorthand notebook. The writing was never automatic. It could be interrupted at any time and later picked up again. Where did the writing come from? It made obvious use of my educational background, interests and experience, but that was in matters of style rather than content. Certainly the subject matter itself was the last thing I would have expected to write about. At several points in the writing the Voice itself speaks in no uncertain terms about the Author (Jesus). *My own reaction to these references, which literally stunned me at the time, have decreased in intensity and are now at the level of mere indecision.*

Psychology was not Helen's only interest and her personality was complex with contradictory traits. She dreaded starting a professional paper, but was equally reluctant to finish one, wanting to revise and polish endlessly. She could sing Melisande's lament from Debussy's opera *Pelleas and Melisande* from memory as well as roles from Gilbert and Sullivan operettas. Although she had few close relationships, those she maintained were intense and sometimes stormy. She did not suffer fools gladly, yet would expend great energy, time, devotion and love in helping others. These often included strangers—and even those she disliked—if they were in need. Her contradictory nature and ambivalence carried over to her feelings about "inner dictation" and A COURSE IN MIRACLES.

It made me very uncomfortable, but it never seriously occurred to me to stop. It seemed to be a special assignment I had somehow, somewhere agreed to complete. It represented a truly collaborative venture between Bill and myself, and much of its significance, I am sure, lies in that. I could neither account for nor reconcile my obviously inconsistent attitudes. On the one hand I still regarded myself as officially an agnostic, resented the material I was taking down, and was strongly impelled to attack it and prove it wrong. On the other hand I spent considerable time in taking it down and later in dictating it to Bill, so it was apparent that I took it quite seriously. I actually came to refer to it as my life's work. As Bill pointed out, I must believe in it if only because I argued with it so much. While this was true, it did not help me. I was in the impossible position of not believing in my own life's work. The situation was clearly ridiculous as well as painful.

During the transmission of A COURSE IN MIRACLES and continuing after its completion, Helen wrote the poems in this volume. Readers familiar with the Course will be aware of the stylistic similarities between the two, as well as their shared spiritual content. Despite these similarities, Helen felt that there was a difference between them. She considered herself the "scribe" of the Course but the "inspired author" of the poems.

The poems were written over a ten-year period. They have been divided into four sections: Early Poems, Personal Poems, Later Poems and The Gifts of God. The actual dates of the poems may be found in the appendix.

The poetry included in the first section dates from March to November of 1971. (There was one earlier poem, "The Gifts of Christmas," which is included with the other Christmas poems in the third section.) These poems were written while Helen was still taking down the Course and deal with spiritual themes found in it.

The personal poems in the second section were written between December, 1973 and February, 1977. They clearly express the ambivalence of Helen's relationship with Jesus: both her love and longing for him, and her fears and wavering faith.

The third section covers a wider span of time—from "The Gifts of Christmas" to Helen's final poem, "The Second Easter," completed in March, 1978. The last poem in this section, "Requiem," was written for a friend whose mother was near death.

The fourth section consists of a long blank verse poem in five sections which is printed here in prose form. It bears a marked similarity to the material in the Course, both in form and content.

Helen chose to conceal her spiritual journey from all but a

few of her closest friends and family members. Others would have been incredulous if they had known of her spiritual writings. While generally ill at ease with the Course, Helen was more uncomfortable and even embarrassed by the poetry, which at times reflects a closer and more personal relationship with Jesus. Because the poems gave Helen's secret away, she did not wish them to be published during her lifetime. In addition, she wanted to preserve her anonymity as "scribe" of A COURSE IN MIRACLES, firmly maintaining that it should stand on its own, with the true author, Jesus, remaining its sole inspirational figure. She knew that any public recognition of her role would distract from this focus. It is only since her death on February 9, 1981, that the Foundation for Inner Peace has decided to publish these poems as its tribute to Helen who gave so much to the world.

*A COURSE IN MIRACLES, Foundation for Inner Peace,
P.O. Box 635, Tiburon, CA 94920

Early Poems

My eyes would look upon the Son of God.
For this I came; to overlook the world,
And seeing it forgiven, understand
Its holiness is but the truth in me.
The Christ walks forth in every step I take.
God shines within me, lighting up the world
In radiant joy. The Holy Spirit comes
With me, lest I should turn and lose the way.
For God has given me a goal to reach,
And has made certain that I cannot fail.
And so He gave me eyes to see beyond
Appearances and shadows. I will see
The Son of God exactly as he is.
And in that sight is all the world transformed,
And blessed forever with the Love of God.

How holy are my footsteps, which but go
To do the Will of God, Whose Son I am.
And how forever perfect is my will,
Which is in no way separate from His Own.

BENEDICTION

Angels are Thoughts that come from God to you.
Secure in their protection may you rest;
Quiet in certainty that comes from them,
At peace in mind and heart and holiness;
Unmindful of the world, and sure that they
Are with you, watching over you, and fixed
In their determination to maintain
Your mind at rest within the peace of God.

THE LAST JUDGMENT

Peace be to you. There is no instant when
You stand alone; no time when God will fail
To take your hand; no moment when His Love
Does not surround you, comfort you and care,
Along with you, for every wish you have,
Each little joy or tiny stab of pain.
At one with you forever, He remains
Your one relationship; your only Friend.
You are the holy Son of God Himself.
Peace be to you, for what is His is yours.

CHRIST'S VISION

Let not the past obscure the now to you.
For thus you waken happily, with joy
Upon your heart and eyes, to see a world
Awaiting to be seen aright at last.
How beautiful the newly-born! For they
Reflect their Father's Love, their brother's care,
The happiness of Heaven, and the peace
That is their true inheritance. It is
On them you look. They have no past today.
All darkness vanishes, and Heaven's smile
Presents a world from which the past is gone,
And present happiness ends all despair
In shining silence and simplicity.

OUR DAILY BREAD

Let me this day arise in quietness
With only thoughts of sinlessness, through which
To look upon the world. Let me today
Behold the world as You would have it be,
Because I am as You created me.
This I accept today. And as the day
Draws to a close, all unforgiving thoughts
Have disappeared, and night comes quietly
To bless a day in quietness begun,
And ending in forgiveness of God's Son.

THE HOLY INSTANT

Each instant celebrates another birth
More perfect than the last, as time goes on
To meet eternity. Yet one can come
Between each instant and the next, to make
The interval a shortening of time
By an immeasurable leap ahead.
How near the goal seems afterwards! How sure
The journey's Guide, how true His words, how pure
The Son of God to whom He speaks. And see
How quickly doubt is lost in certainty.

THE HOLY PURPOSE

There is no death. What God creates must be
Eternal, changeless, incorruptible
And safe forever. Can the holy die?
And can the Son of God be made as he
Was not created? Heed the body not.
It serves its purpose and is given up.
It cannot suffer if the mind invests
It with a holy purpose. Miracles
Are always ready to restore and heal
The mind's intent, if it forget its goal.
Communication, then restored, will be
The Holy Spirit's single remedy.

There is a silence and a certainty
Apart from time; a peace and quietness
Surrounded by a thousand angels' wings,
And kept inviolate by God's Own Hand.
It is for everyone. Yet very few
Have found it. It will wait for everyone
Who seek, and all of them will find at last
This secret haven, hidden from the world,
And yet in open sight. Its clarity
Is blazing, yet it is not often seen.
Its call is constant, yet is rarely heard.
Attack must overlook it, yet to love
It gives an instant answer. Here the Will
Of God is recognized and cherished still.
And it is here that finally God's Son
Will understand his will and God's are one.

The wish to harm alone engenders fear.
Without it is protection obvious,
And shelter offered everywhere. There is
No time when safety need be sought, no place
Where it is absent, and no circumstance
Which can endanger it in any way.
It is secured by every loving thought,
Made more apparent by each loving glance,
Brought nearer by forgiving words, and kept
Untroubled, cloudless, open to the light,
Redeemed, restored and holy in Christ's sight.

Where stars are formless but their light remains,
And shines forever; where the sun has lost
Its burning heat, and yet it still retains
A gentle and eternal glow that keeps
All things in peace and softness, and the rays
From every living thing reach out to find
All other living things, and on from them
To their Creator; where, when petals fall
And leaves decay, the scent and color of
The flowers come, preserved forever fresh
And lovely, and the song of birds remains
Although their wings are still; here everyone
Will come to rest, his journey almost done,
And hears God's Voice acknowledging His Son.

THE HOLY RELATIONSHIP

I am God's Son, His mother, father, friend,
His brother and His love. For all of this
Is He to me, and thus am I to Him.
The world is His. And being His is mine.
My holiness extends from Him, to be
His holiness, by love complete in me.

THE SONG OF PEACE

The melody of peace is always there.
It neither dies nor wavers. It remains
A calm, soft sound, more still than silence, and
An ageless recollection in the minds
That God created. Ceaselessly it sings
To all the world, that it remember Him.
The sounds of earth are quieted before
This ancient melody, which speaks of love
In limitless dimensions. Where is fear,
When God has guaranteed that He is here?

THE FACE OF CHRIST

The face of Christ is wholly innocent.
He never looked on sin, nor felt the pain
Of condemnation and attack. Serene
As God's creation, and as surely held
Within the golden circle of God's Love,
The face of Christ has never known a tear,
Nor looked upon illusions. His the calm
That God intended for His holy Son,
Who was and is and will be only one.

ALTERNATIVES

A fantasy of pain, a dream of death,
A cry of agony, a shallow breath,
Such is the world you see. Is this your choice
To be the substitution for God's Voice?
There is an Answer to all questions here,
An instant when the world will disappear.
Perceptions pass, however sure they seem,
For Christ has put His ending on the dream.

THE CALL OF CHRIST

We have a real relationship,
The Christ and I.
He shines on me from every face,
And every flower brings His grace.
I call to Him when I forget,
And He remembers, and will let
Me have His thoughts instead of mine.
And in His face I see the sign
Of resurrection and release;
Of perfect holiness and peace.
All that I see in Him I see
With equal certainty in me.
He lives in our relationship,
And so do I.

THY KINGDOM COME

There is no answer to the Voice for God
Except His Word.
There is no sound except the Voice for God
That can be heard.
For this His Son has ears; to hear God's Will,
And let the ego's voice at last be still.

CORRECTION

Let me not recollect my past mistakes,
Nor call them sins. My errors wait upon
Correction. That is all. There is no past,
For real correction is beyond all time,
All place, all circumstance, and every thought
That seems to be a sin. Therefore am I
Absolved and wholly innocent. Mistakes
Have disappeared, without imprint or trace
Upon the shining glory of Christ's face.

REDEMPTION

My brother sleeps because I see him not.
His restless dreams have drawn the lines of pain
Deeply across his forehead, and his tears
Are dampening his fevered cheeks. He twists
And turns in silent agony. He is
My savior crucified. And he will wait
Until I see Christ's face in him, to be
Awakened and redeemed, along with me.

THE PROMISE

Hear me, my Lord! I cannot call in vain.
Such is Your promise. I but do Your Will
To call on You. And You will answer me,
Because Your promise holds the Answer still.

Throughout the years, throughout the arc of time,
What was still is, and yet will be again;
Your single promise, never to be changed.
Hear me, my Lord! I cannot call in vain.

THE LITTLE THINGS OF GOD

Gardens are filled with little things of God
That sing and twitter in a tiny voice,
And flash from blade to blade across the grass.
They shine with morning and they glow at night,
And through the daylight wind and hum and turn,
Wheeling among the flowers as they live
Their little lives, and then they disappear.
Yet when they enter in eternity,
They will be part of God along with me.

THE CIRCULAR WAY

The transient things are not of God. For He
Creates like to Himself. How could it be
That what the One Eternal calls His Own
Has but a little life, with breath on loan
And mortgaged unto death? We seem to go
From birth to certain death, and do not know
What goes before or after. Yet we tread
A golden circle, and are surely led
Back to the Source of our infinity,
To which we will return as certainty.

QUIETNESS

The world knows not of quiet. Restlessness
Is its abiding law. From there it goes
To pain and joylessness, and back again
To the unceasing restlessness on which
It stands, uncertain, insecure and frail,
Prey to illusions, victimized by guilt.
Yet quietness comes over it at last.
For when forgiveness comes, its certain gift
Is stillness, in which all the world is hushed;
A silence where the littleness of sin
Shrinks into nothingness before the Love
Forgiveness represents. And in His Name
Is everyone acknowledged as the same.

RENUNCIATION

You are not asked to sacrifice the good
Or the desirable in any way.
You are asked only to renounce all things
That would destroy your peace. For God is Love.
Center your thoughts on Him, and you will see
He gives you everything, with neither more
Nor less conceivable from this time forth,
And on to the eternal. Sorrow is
Inaccurate perception; pain is but
A sad mistake. Renounce but this, and you
Call unto Christ to pardon and renew.

DEFINITION

The temporary is of time,
By definition.
God's is the everlasting. His the Call
From the eternal, still abode of all
Whom He created, to return in peace
To Heaven and tranquility, and cease
The senseless journey to attain an aim
That stands for nothing, and that has no name.
For timeless things belong to Him,
By definition.

IDENTITY

Be still an instant. Draw aside the veil.
Look beyond seeming. Here there is a place,
A borderland between perception and
The certain knowledge of the Mind of God.
Here do they meet and blend an instant more,
Until perception fades and disappears,
And only the Eternal still remains.
Forgiveness has removed all else but Him,
And therefore there is nothing else but You.

GOD'S LIKENESS

How holy are you, Son of God! How pure
Your thoughts; how innocent your mind. In you
I see the Host of God; His Love, His Joy,
His one creation, indivisible.
You are as like to God as I to you,
And being like to you, I am like Him.

Love is the angels' gift, received from God.
They hover over you and lay their gifts
Gently before your feet, and shower them
Along your path whichever way you go,
Paving the road with silver, so your steps
Leave shining footprints, marking out the way
You go to God. Who follows on this path
The angels bless with gifts, along with you.
And everyone who stores their gifts as his,
Adds what he has received to what you gave
And what you have received. For angels' gifts
Increase with giving. They return to God
Your treasure house, and then come back to you
With all His gratitude. For those who walk
With you become God's angels here on earth,
And he to whom you pointed out the way,
Becomes the messenger from God to you.

THE CHRIST THOUGHT

Hold to the Thought the Christ has placed in you.
This was the Thought which came with you, and gives
Your coming all the purpose that it has.
You have no function but to find this Thought,
To recognize it and to see it as
Your chosen wish, while wishes still prevail,
And the reflection of the Will of God,
Which also is your will. Till that is known,
Accept Christ's Thought, and let it be your own.

THE GREETING

Say but "I love you" to all living things,
And they will lay their blessing over you
To keep you ever safe and ever sure
That you belong to God and He to you.

What but "I love you" could the greeting be
Of Christ to Christ, Who welcomes but Himself?
And what are you except the Son of God,
The Christ Whom He would welcome to Himself?

CHRIST'S NEED

He needs my voice. He needs my hands and feet.
He needs my eyes to look upon and bless
Our tired brothers, weary of the world,
And yet believing it is all there is.
How can they learn except He teach through me?
How can He give them hope but through my voice?
How can I hear His Voice except through them?

THE FINAL VISION

When silence settles all across the world,
No living thing but stillness holds its heart
In rapt anticipation, and the peace
Foretold so long ago at last has come.
Only the face of Christ will still be seen
Upon a world which, in an instant more,
Will sink from memory without a sign
It ever was. Where is perception when
The Voice for God has said the last amen?

There is no light in all the world but seems
To dwindle into darkness, as the light
Of truth is lit and spreads across the world.
There is no thought in all the world but fades
To meaningless obscurity, as peace
Lays all the thinking of the world to rest
Before the altar to the Word of God.
And there will be no epitaphs upon
A world that never was, when sight is done
And hearing left behind. Atonement seals
The book of days and hours. With the dream
Of death and separation laid aside,
In deepest silence and serenity
The mind God loves is still at last in Him.

Who would dream now? What wish is unfulfilled?
What is there God has not already willed?

THE MIRRORS OF CHRIST

A breeze comes by. A little lake jumps up,
Sparkles a shining instant and is still.
A brook skips down the hillside, and is held
Within the cup the joining mountains fill.
A pond is ruffled for an instant as
A storm upsets its smoothness, and returns
To its accustomed quietness. The sea
Dives deeply downward swirling, and upturns
To catch the moon. So all things come to peace,
Away from turbulence and from the past,
United in salvation, to become
The silent mirrors of Christ's face at last.

THE ARCH OF SILENCE

The love of Heaven arches over me
In perfect quiet. Nothing from the world
Can reach within its stillness. There can be
No sharp intruders and no witnesses
To unreality. The simple might
Of innocence alone is there. Pretense
Of any kind has fallen out of sight.
In honest clarity the world appears,
Redeemed and wakened from the dream of tears.

THE INNER LIGHT

The time will come when time is meaningless,
And place is nowhere. All our concepts wait
But their appointed ending. They uphold
A dream with no dimensions. At the gate
Of Heaven are they merely laid aside,
Before the blazing of the light within.

THE JOINING

Peace to the Son of God. What else could be
His Father's Will for him? And what but this
Could he receive? What other gifts are there
He could be offered, and accept as his?
Peace is his holy need. In this his wish
Soars to the holy height of Heaven's Will,
Hovers an instant, settles and is still.

ANGER IS DONE

Anger is done. Forever there will be
No more attack. No one will cry in pain.
No one will grieve. Nor thorns be placed again
Around the holy head of God's Own Son.
Safe in the stillness of reality,
Where time has disappeared and space has gone,
Open your eyes, you holy Son of God.
You came to look on this. Anger is done.

THE CERTAIN HELP

Our Brother shows the way. We follow Him,
For He will not betray our little hope,
Our wandering footsteps and our shreds of faith;
Our tiny trust and our uncertain call.
Beside our pitiful appeals, He lays
His mighty power, given Him by God,
Which neither manger nor the cross could hold.
Our resurrection is as sure as His,
For in His resurrection is our own.

There is a singing underneath the world
That holds it up, and enters in behind
All twisted thoughts, and comes to set them straight.
There is an ancient melody that still
Abides in every mind and sings of peace,
Eternity, and all the quiet things
That God created. Angels sing with joy,
And offer you their song, for it is yours.
You sing as ceaselessly. The Son of God
Can never sing alone. His voice is shared
By all the universe. It is the call
To God, and answered by His Voice Itself.

Redemption is a very quiet thing.
The noises of the world are still before
Its gentle advent. Silently it comes,
Asking for nothing; giving everything.
Its quietness extends across the world,
And stops just short of Heaven, where there is
No further need for anything at all.
Without demands the Son of God can rest,
Accepting what belongs to him in truth.
Now is he silent. Now his mind is still.
Now does he recognize what is his will.

To heal it is not needful to allow
The thought of bodies to engulf your mind
In darkness and illusions. Healing is
Escape from all such thoughts. You hold instead
Only a single thought, which teaches you
Your brother is united with your mind,
So bodily intrusions on his peace
Cannot arise to jeopardize the Son
Whom God created sinless as Himself.
Think never of the body. Healing is
The thought of unity. Forget all things
That seem to separate. Your brother's pain
Has but one remedy; the same as yours.
He must be whole, because he joins with you,
And you are healed, because you join with him.

MORNING

How lovely is the morning! All the things
Of earth are fresh and newly born again.
The ravages that seemed to wear away
The newness in which yesterday began
Have been restored. The world's recovery
Shines on each blade of grass and every leaf
That sings again of morning. And God's Voice
Calls to His Son to make another choice.

THE ETERNAL SAFETY

Holy am I. By Love created, and
By Love sustained. For I have never left
The Everlasting Arms. I am beset
By dreams of sin, and grim forebodings seem
To steal away my peace, and leave me prey
To terror and malignant destiny.
Yet does my holiness remain untouched,
As God created it. For there can be
No sin in God, and therefore none in me.

Choose once again. For it is given you
To trail the peace of God across the world
Without exception. Every child receives
The gifts you bring, and men and women turn
To you in thankfulness. With joy are you
Accepted everywhere. For you have come
Only to bring Infinity's appeal
To those who are as infinite as He.
You come with memory of God in you,
To waken this same memory in those
In whom it seems to sleep. The world would die
Without its saviors. Do not, then, deny
Your proper place. For Christ has called to you
To follow Him, and choose the silent way
That brings you to eternity today.

I cannot fail in anything. I am
Supported by the angels, led by God
Unto Himself. The Christ establishes
My own Identity as His. The love
Of all God's universe belongs to me.
What place has sorrow in my universe
When it is but a mirror for what God
Created as forever filled with joy?
Forgiveness is the mirror of His Love,
And it is this I would hold out to Him,
To catch the dream of holiness He gives,
And then to find that it is not a dream.

THE CERTAIN WAY

I walk in holiness. My way is sure
In spite of all my doubts. I do not make
My own direction. Nor can I endow
My mind with guidance that can teach me how
To save me from illusions. Only God
Offers Atonement that is sure to save.
Only the Father knows what gifts He gave.

THE SIGN

We bow not to Your Will, for it is ours.
What but a glad acceptance could we feel
When we have recognized that, in Your Love,
What had been made to hurt is used to heal,
As our united will is recognized?
Our brothers are beside us. And as we
Were one in our creation, as we come
To understand forgiveness, we will see
The gap between us fade to nothingness.
Our joined hands here reflect the state of mind
Where Heaven is remembered. This the sign
That Your salvation is not far behind.

THE TIMELESS GIFTS

All things that God created timeless are
His gifts to me. The passing and the frail
Are not a part of my inheritance.
Such are His promises. He cannot fail
To keep them perfectly. His sacred Word
Is given me in silence. I will trust
In Him because I listened and I heard.

HIS CERTAINTY

I come in doubt. I do not yet believe
Your promises. My own uncertainty
Seems to be more apparent than my faith
In What You have ordained Your Son must be,
And how Your memory returns to him.
My steps are hesitant, my trust is weak,
My sense of purpose falters. I forget
My goal because of images I seek,
And wander in illusions. Yet the end
Of wandering is certain in Your Mind;
What You would have me seek, that will I find.

THEY WAIT

I did not know Your Voice. And what I heard
I did not understand. There was a Word
In which was everything. Yet all I found
In its immensity was but the sound
Of meaningless contention. I passed by
A thousand waiting angels. And as I
Rushed along vain detours I did not see
The hosts of holiness surrounding me.
Yet I will certainly return. For You
Have promised that whatever I may do,
Angels and holy hosts will wait; the Word
Will hover over me till it is heard.

Let us not question, but be still a while.
There is an answer given us before
We ask the question; a solution to
All strife and pain and turbulence; a door
To silence and to absolution. We
Are free before we ask for freedom, healed
Before we ask for healing; remedy
For every sorrow given us, and sealed
Within us, always present, always near,
In easy access, readily made plain.
God's Son is answered. Wearily at last,
He calls upon his Father's Name again.

Ours is a common task. Each one is called,
And he will answer as he makes the choice
To give up madness, and to choose instead
To recognize and to accept God's Voice.
Each one will waken at the time and place
That he has chosen, and will take his part
In the Atonement's purpose. For he came
With resurrection's calling in his heart.
He must attain a glorious rebirth,
And scatter stars across the sleeping earth.

THE LITTLE GIFT

Let it be so. Our willingness is all
Salvation asks. We could not find a gift
So tiny yet so mighty; one which has
The power to awake God's Son, and lift
His heart to Heaven. Be it as God wills,
And nothing still remains to block the light
From entering where God would have it be,
And shimmer up to greet Christ's holy sight.

STILLNESS

My soul is still. It does not know the thoughts
My mind imagines. It does not perceive
My meaningless endeavors, nor the goals
Of sin and madness in which I believe.
Immovable my soul remains, and sure
Of immortality, in peace so deep
That all the shocks I feel can not come near
Its limitless tranquility. I sleep,
And dream of evil and decay and death,
Of which my soul knows nothing. Perfectly
It rests in its Creator and in me.

My tiny empire is no fitting gift
For God's most holy Son. His Father gives
Him infinite dominion and estate
Unlimited, extending outward to
Embrace the universe. My world contracts
To nothingness, where thoughtless images
Dance wearily an instant and are gone.
What can I offer Him Who came to save
Me from the world I made, except Himself?
For there remains within me still one gift
That yet is worthy to be given Him.
Let me forgive myself. For that is all
He asks and needs. And He will take this gift,
And bring it to His Father from Himself.

I cannot be replaced. I am unique
In God's creation. I am held so dear
By Him that it is madness to believe
That I could suffer pain or loss or fear.
Holy am I; in sinlessness complete,
In wisdom infinite, in love secure,
In patience perfect, and in faithfulness
Beyond all thought of sin, and wholly pure.
Who could conceive of suffering for me?
Surely the mind that thought it is insane.
I never left my Father's house. What need
Have I to journey back to Him again?

THE TINY INSTANT

This tiny instant, briefer than a dream,
And like a dream as well, I call my life.
It holds no reason I can call upon,
Nor an escape from its incessant strife.
It has no goal nor purpose. It is vain
In every aspect and in every way.
Yet God has given judgment otherwise.
I did not see the glory for the clay.
I saw the shadows but I missed the sun.
My thoughts were false and my perception dim.
What is my life except a link within
An endless chain that reaches up to Him?

Personal Poems

Strange was my Love to me. For when He came
I did not know Him. And He seemed to me
To be but an intruder on my peace.
I did not see the gifts He brought, nor hear
His soft appeal. I tried to shut Him out
With locks and keys that merely fell away
Before His coming. I could not escape
The gentleness with which He looked at me.
I asked Him in unwillingly, and turned
Away from Him. But He held out His hand
And asked me to remember Him. In me
An ancient Name began to stir and break
Across my mind in gold. The light embraced
Me deep in silence till He spoke the Word,
And then at last I recognized my Lord.

Love, You are silent. Not one shining word
Has reached my heart for an eternity
Of waiting and of tears. I have forgot
Your face that once was everything to me,
But now is almost nothing. What You were
I do but half remember. What You are
I do not know at all. What You will be
Is unimagined. Sometimes I believe
I knew You once. And then again I think
You were a dream that once I thought was real.

My eyes are closing, Love. Without Your Word
I will but sleep, and sleeping will forget
Even the dream. Is silence what You gave
In golden promise as the Son of God?
Is this bleak unresponsive shadowland
The overcoming that You offered those
Who understood the Father through the Son?
Is endless distance what must stand between
My Love and me? You promised that You will
Forever answer. Yet, Love, You are still.

I have betrayed my God in many ways,
Throughout the bitter nights and secret days.
My hate drove deep into my mind, and tore
Away the little love I had in store.
I watched it go without regret, for I
Did not perceive how much I lost thereby.
With hatred as a friend, I did not fear
To lose it for a god I held more dear.
For now I seemed secure, by hate held fast,
And feeling I was safe from love at last.

The eyes of Christ looked steadily on me
As if my secret hate He did not see.
I hugged it tight and hid it in my heart,
And still I held it from His Love apart.
Until one day my eyes met His, and then
My fingers opened and my heart. And when
I looked away a star was in my hand;
Another in my heart. I listened, and
His voice said silently to me, "Now go
And hate no more." And I said, "Be it so."

O You who came in winter and who left
Among the lilies, stay with me and fill
My eyes with glory, and my heart with love
That smiles forever on the world You saw,
And that You loved as You would have me love.
For with this vision I will look on You,
And recognize my Savior in all things
I did not understand. Now is the world
Reborn in me because I share Your Love.
Now in my healed and holy mind there dawns
The memory of God. And now I rise
To Him in all the loveliness I knew
When I was first created one with You.

THE LAST PRAYER

Hold out Your hand, my Lord. I am not far
From home. But still I do not see the way
As yet. I hear Your Voice as little but
A tiny whisper sometimes heard, but far
More often silent. And the sight of You
Is but a spark that lights the darkness for
An instant and goes out. Perhaps Your Voice
Is nothing but the rustle of the wind
Around dead leaves. Perhaps the sparks I think
Are the beginning of the sight of You
Are matches struck in darkness. It may be
There is no home that I am coming to;
There is no way that I can reach to You.

O You who promised that You are the Way,
The Truth, the Life, and all things hoped for, come
And steady me the little journey more
That yet remains untravelled and unsure.
Doubt drags my feet from hastening to You,
My little faith is faltering and dim,
And flickers like a candle going out.
Alone it will not last the little way
I yet must go. Perhaps I merely dreamed
You stood in glory waiting till I came
And sank into the Everlasting Arms.
Hold out Your hand at last, my Lord, to me,
And lift me to the final Certainty.

"Come unto Me," He said. And I replied,
"I would indeed, if only I could see
Who calls and where He is. I do not know
Who speaks to me. Nor do I understand
What He would have me do." A little light
Shines briefly in the dark, and I forget
Even the place where for an instant it
Laced through the blackness and then disappeared.

You call, but it is not enough to hear
A voice unplaced, however sweet it be,
However urgently it may appeal,
However strong its pull against my heart.
My time grows thin, and yet it is not time.
I wait with failing breath and hope but this:
When You appear no doubt is possible,
And I must come, for I will be like You.

Enter my house. Its holiness is Yours,
And it must wait for You who are the home
Of Holiness Itself. Its altar stands
Darkened as yet, but open to the light
That You will bring. I have forgot the glow
Of diamonds and the glittering of gold
That once I thought would lighten up the dark
And bring me comfort. Silvered drapes are gone,
And floors are empty of the heavy rugs
That once concealed their bareness with designs
That Eastern hands had woven carefully
In thick obscurity. Their bareness is
The sign the Guest that was to come is yet
Not ready to appear, and bring the peace
That He has promised those who dwell with Him.
My ringless fingers hold a lamp long since
Gone out and cold. The wind sings bitterly
A chant of fear that echoes round the walls
And enters ceaselessly into my heart.

This was supposed to be a temple built
To You who said the altar would be lit
Forever. And I thought that You had said
A holy altar cannot be a tomb.

I tarry by the wayside. Homeless I
Return each evening to an empty house
But to awaken and return each day,
To wait again in silence and despair.
How long, O Lord, did You ordain I be
A dweller in a ghost-house? Shadows come
And fall across my eyes at night, to bring
A parody of sleep. By day I go
In an illusion that I am awake
To my appointed round of bitterness.
The cup from which I drink is empty. And
The crumbs allotted me will not sustain
My little life but shortly. I retain
A hope so frail it stifles in the dust
Of waiting on an ancient way that seems
To lead to nowhere. I have not forgot
Your promise. I will wait until You come.
But I must wait in sorrow, with the song
Of dying all around me on the road
On which I stand and wait for Your return.
How long, O lovely Lord of Life, how long?

I have no other gods. But yesterday
I gave the last away. The world has gone
From the last inventory I would make
And offer You. The paper has no marks
Upon its whiteness. On Your altar I
Lay nothing, for it should remain as You
Created it and still would have it be.

With nothing for support I turn to You,
Though not in certainty. The world I shed
Was all I knew and all I understood.
Perhaps I was mistaken in the hope
That You would lift my heart and fill my hands,
When I would come without the gods I made,
With nothing left to keep apart from You.

I did not think that I could be deceived,
Although I feared it might be so. I thought
My gods had less and less to give, until
I hardly cared to rise to their defense.
Yet now I stand uncertain, offering
Only my doubts, my unsure faith and hope,
Even the thought, "But what if You should fail?"

Waiting is terrible. And yet I know
That I have waited many times before.
In vanity and hopelessness I go
From dark to darker and to darkest door.

And yet there is a difference. For I hear
Another voice, still faint, perhaps, that sings
An ancient melody. The cries of fear
Are slightly softened by the stir of wings.

Maybe there is an end to waiting. He
Who promised to return may yet arise
From what appeared as death. He still may be
What never was begun and never dies.

Perhaps there was a time, so long ago
It is not half remembered, when I fled,
Too soon to see the fearful shadows go,
And look upon the living, not the dead.

Let me not lose the tiny spark of trust
That sprang to sudden life so lately born.
Perhaps the living never fell to dust.
Perhaps there never was a need to mourn.

Let me remember. For it yet may be
It was not as I thought. The dying rose,
And maybe, in my haste, I did not see
A circle not begun needs not to close.

My Lord, my Love, my Life, I live in you.
There is no life apart from what you are.
I breathe your words, I rest upon your arms.
My sight is hallowed by your single star.

I do not always recognize your face,
Or hear your Voice. I do not always see
The strangers whom you send are messengers
You choose to bring your holy Word to me.

You are the stranger then. And I am dead
To holy things that Heaven's light shines through.
The world I see is enemy to me
When I forget my lovely Love is you.

Forgetting you is to forget myself,
Why I have come and where it is I go.
My Lord, my Love, my Life, let me forget
All things except the loveliness you know.

My arms are open. Come, my Lord, to me
And rest upon my heart. It beats for you
And sings in joyous welcome. What am I
Except your resting place and your repose?

Your rest is mine. Without you I am lost
In senseless wanderings that have no end,
No goal, no meaning, on a road that goes
In twisted byways down to nothingness.

Come now, my Love, and save me from despair.
The Way, the Truth, the Life are with me then.
The journey is forgotten in the joy
Of endless quiet and your kiss of peace.

Lead me, my Lord, to where my stillness is.
I seek my Father's Everlasting Arms
Which I alone can never hope to find,
For I am frail in seeking and in love.

Idols will come to hold their halting hands
Before me on my lonely journeying
Which will forever bar the way to me,
And I will faint in an illusion's grasp.

But come you with me and I cannot fail
To find my Father's house. As we approach
The holy gate, illusions shudder back
And angels come to offer us their wings.

I am the least and yet the greatest. I
Who hold your hand have Heaven's might with me.
I go in glory, for you walk with me.
Deliver me into my Father's Arms.

Later Poems

Hallowed my name. I am a Son of God
Who walks in stillness. I hold out my hand,
And from my fingertips the quiet goes
Around the world to still all living things,
And cover them in holiness. Their rest
Is joined in mine, for I am one with them.
There is no pain my stillness cannot heal,
Because it comes from God. There is no grief
That does not turn to laughter when I come.
I do not come alone. There walks with me
The Light that Heaven looks on as itself.
I am a Son of God. My name is His.
My Father's house is where my stillness is.

Forget not time was made for you, not you
For time. The withered, dying and the dead
Are but the thoughts of those who do not see
That time is powerless, unless they give
Their own consent to change. The Son of God
Stands changelessly within Unchangingness,
Past the ephemeral, not new nor old,
Beyond all opposites, where nothing casts
A shadow or a doubt, for light alone
Surrounds him. Time was given him to show
Him how to learn and see, and then to know.

There is a silence that betrays the Christ
Because the Word of God remains unheard
By those in bitter need. Unspoken still
The Word salvation holds for them, and kept
Away their resurrection from a world
That is but hell and alien to God's Son.
Homeless they wander, nowhere finding peace,
Unknown, unknowing, blind in darkness, and
Unborn within the silence of the tomb.

There is a silence into which God's Word
Has poured an ancient meaning, and is still.
Nothing remains unsaid nor unreceived.
Strange dreams are washed in golden water from
The blazing silence of the peace of God,
And what was evil suddenly becomes
The gift of Christ to those who call on Him.
His final gift is nothing but a dream,
Yet in that single dream is dreaming done.

What seems to be a birth is but a step
From timelessness to time. The peace of God
Shines down upon a manger and a cross
In equal silence. Neither one will last.
The dream of a beginning and an end
Can never touch God's Son. He seemed to take
A human form and then he seemed to die.
There is no death because there is no birth.
The crucified is risen up to God.

Salvation is as plain as open day.
Its unambiguous simplicity
Is far beyond distortion or misuse.
It cannot be betrayed nor reconciled
With error and attack. It never fails
In its forgiving gentleness. It stands
Like to a mother holding out her arms
To tired children, asking them to come
And rest in her protection. Do not think
The darkness in your heart has banished you
From the eternal home your Father set
Among the stars for you. What you betrayed
Was never there to suffer from the hurts
You thought you gave. And all the things you stole
Were glittering illusions; all your thoughts
Of murder and abuse, of death and pain,
Of sickness, loss and misery, were but
The dreams of fever. Holy Son of God,
Your innocence is unassailable
Because of what you are. Salvation states
The simple truth: The Son of God is free,
Because he is as God would have him be.

There is an end to sorrow. What was made
Will be unmade. The transient toys of spite
Will turn to dust. The things of time will fade
And vanish into nothingness. The night
Of evil dreams will gently yield to light.

All things that God created not will close
As they began, in secret and in shame
Which, never being born, cannot oppose
God's holy Will to let forgiveness frame
The face of Christ, Who enters in His Name.

What need we do to let forgiveness come?
Nothing. We need but realize that we
And all the world together are the sum
Of all salvation's promise. I am he
Who speaks God's Word, and you along with me.

There is an end to sorrow. In God's Will
The Christ serenely rests. God's holy Son
Is all creation is, for he is still
As God created him. Forever one,
His Word is changeless; spoken, it is done.

The flicker of an instant stands between
Us and complete salvation. Need we do
More than God asks? The face of Christ is seen
And then unseen forever. Sorrow too
Has disappeared, and I along with you.

It happens suddenly. There is a Voice
That speaks one Word, and everything is changed.

You understand an ancient parable
That seemed to be obscure. And yet it meant
Exactly what it said. The trivial
Enlarge in magnitude, while what seemed large
Resumes the littleness that is its due.
The dim grow bright, and what was bright before
Flickers and fades and finally is gone.
All things assume the role that was assigned
Before time was, in ancient harmony
That sings of Heaven in compelling tones
Which wipe away the doubting and the care
All other roles convey. For certainty
Must be of God.

It happens suddenly,
And all things change. The rhythm of the world
Shifts into concert. What was harsh before
And seemed to speak of death now sings of life,
And joins the chorus to eternity.
Eyes that were blind begin to see, and ears
Long deaf to melody begin to hear.
Into the sudden stillness is reborn
The ancient singing of creation's song,
Long silenced but remembered. By the tomb
The angel stands in shining hopefulness
To give salvation's message: "Be you free,
And stay not here. Go on to Galilee."

Help me forgive the world, my Lord. For then
The quiet comes in which the dream is done.
The wanderer comes home, the lame arise,
The sightless see. For fear cannot approach
The wholly sinless world forgiveness sees.
Let its soft light awaken sight in me,
And seeing, let the dream of fear be gone.

I have no choice but to forgive the world.
The dream that peace can come another way
Is sick illusion. Christ accepts a dream
His Father shines upon. Behold this dream;
It is His gift to me. Look on a world
So gentle and so still no leaf can fall,
And not one blade of grass can be destroyed.

There is a light that shines upon this world,
And judges it as Christ would have it judged.
There is no condemnation on it. He
Beholds it sinless, in the light that shines
From His Own face. His vision looks upon
The sure reflection of His Father's Love;
The picture calling up His memory.

What can remain of evil in the world
Christ's vision looks upon? And what could still
Appear to me as fearful, with the light
Of His perfection on it? What could teach
Me sorrow has a cause, or death is real?
Help me forgive the world. The peace You give
In my forgiveness will be given me.

The world can be to us a shining star,
Because it represents a Thought of God.
In truth it has no form. But seen in time
It lies between His fingers, and is still
Within the sure protection of His hand.
His face shines down on it, and in response
It sparkles up to Him. There is no care
In anyone who dwells upon the land
His hand has covered, and His Voice assures
Of everlasting holiness and peace.
His Son abides where He would have him be.
And not one beat in Heaven's song is missed
Within the quiet shining of the star
That is the silent Answer to the quest
The world has set, but which does not exist.

When it is recognized there is no quest,
No hand, no Voice, no Answer, and no thought
Apart from God, the star will disappear.
For what it now reflects will take its place
For just one instant more. And then the dream
That is the world is over. Sun and moon
And all the stars are happy thoughts with which
The sad illusion of the world is lit
And interlaced. The star that is the form
It takes until the One Creator is
Accepted as the Source of everything,
Is not eternal. Yet the Light of God
Still shines on it, until there is no time
And stars have vanished. Then the stillness comes
In which there is no form, no sound, no dream.

There was a cross, but it has disappeared.
There was a world, but there is only God.

Father, Your child is crying in the night
Because she thinks that she is all alone
In darkness and in fear. She does not know
That You are watching still. Send her Your Voice
To speak in stillness deep as summer fields
Kept windless in the blazing sun of noon
And silvered in the silence of the night,
But yet as loud as thunder. Tell her that
She need but turn to You, and You will come
So swiftly she will instantly forget
The years or minutes her Identity
In You was unremembered. Who could then
Recall the tiny ticks of time in which
The past went by; the fearful thoughts in which
The future was kept carefully concealed
In black unknowingness? Eternity
Has come to lift them both away, and shine
In quiet certainty in place of time,
And all the little things that time must bring.
Look now upon the child who has forgot
The meaning of creation. You alone
Can save what she has damned. Yet all her thoughts
Return to dust when Yours have come to her.

O holy Father of the universe,
Creator of all things that live in You,
In Whom not one could ever be forgot
Nor lost in time, the dreaming of the world
Will pass away with Your rememberance.
No child of Yours but must remember You.
Yet time obscures eternity, as truth

Seems to be hidden when illusions rise
And veil the face of Christ. It does not seem
To have reality, and You Who are
More near than breathing yet appear to be
Remote, unreal, so far the distant stars
Seem closer. In long darkness it is hard
To keep the faith in the returning sun.
Your child is tired. Let her hear Your Voice,
And rest that sleep can never give is hers.
Your child is sad. Remind her of Your Word,
And all the joy that suddenly becomes
Your gift to her is shared by all the world.
She is afraid. But let her hear the sound
Of Heaven's reassurance, and the years
Of almost hopeless waiting and despair
Shrink to a holy instant and are gone.

You do not want our praise. You want our love,
For praise is merely words. You want instead
Our gentle blessing on those You would save
And shelter in Your Arms. You want our care
For them as part of You and of ourselves,
To teach us that the Son of God is whole,
And cannot be cut off from what is his.
You do not want our grief. You want our joy
To share with all the world, already made
Too sorrowful. And should we offer You
A useless gift You would not give the world?
We give to You, and You return to us
A greater gift, so infinitely more
We scarce can understand its magnitude.
Yet must we give before we can receive,
For You can but increase the gifts we give
Before they are returned to us again.

Our joint endeavor is salvation's task.
You are the Answer; we the ones who ask.

Step back, My child, and let Him lead the way
Whom I have sent to you. He holds your hand
And speaks to you of Me. His memory
Holds in your mind My Name. His peace surrounds
My child with all the love a Father feels
For what He cherishes above all else
In earth and Heaven. Whom I sent to you
Has shared My Heart and brings My Word with Him
To solace and to comfort all the world
That has forgot My Name. Homeless are they
Who would abide alone, apart from Me.
Yet would I call them home. My Voice I send
To sing in soundless places. Hear from Me
The song a Father sings to you, His child;
A melody from far beyond the world.
Step back and listen, for He comes to bless
And tell you that you are not comfortless.

Be still, my soul, and rest upon the Lord
In quiet certainty. For He has come
To rescue you from doubt. And now you stand
In blazing glory of a risen sun
That cannot set. It will forever be
Exactly as it is. You stand with Him
Within a radiance prepared for you
Before time was and far beyond its reach.
Be still and know. And knowing, be you sure
Your Lord has come to you. There is no doubt
That stands before His countenance, nor can
Conceal from you what He would have you see.
The sun has risen. He has come at last.
Where stands His Presence there can be no past.
Be still, my soul, and rest upon the Lord
Who comes to keep the promise of His Word.

Peace cover you, within without the same,
In shining silence and in peace so deep
No dream of sin and evil can come near
Your quiet mind. And then in stillness wake.
First there is silence; then awakening.
Now is the time appointed for the end
Of dreaming. Still the cradle where you come
To be reborn. The Christ is stirring in
The home that He has chosen as His Own.
His vision rests upon your eyes, and soon
You will behold His face, and will forget
The fantasies that seemed to be so real
Until the stillness came. The Son of God
Has come to join you now. His shining hand
Is on your shoulder. And God's silent Voice
Speaks ceaselessly of Heaven. You will hear
His single message calling to His Own
From His abiding place, to wake in God.

Cherish this instant. All of time is set
Within its boundaries. The past but led
To this appointed time. The future yet
Remains unborn, and like a word unsaid
Is soundless. Seek instead the endless place
Of timelessness. In unencumbered space
Open your arms to let all conflict cease,
And call to quiet those in every place
Who wait for freedom. You would not betray
Their agony and patience, when their cries
Fade into silence here. For Christ will stay
Until the faint and final echo dies
And stillness claims the world. And then He takes
It in His hand and waits an instant more,
And time is over. Even now He makes
Your way to Him. This instant is the door
To that in which the world will disappear
In Him, as He will vanish into One
Who will remain forever. In this clear
And shining instant all of time is done.

Let us forget the dark and hurtful ways
We travelled on with you; the twisted feet
That walked against the holy Will of God,
Away from peace and from the quiet lake
That was the resting place that He ordained.
The fumbling, failing creature has become
The gift of God. In holy thankfulness
We see in you what each of us can be
And will become with you. You chose for us,
And turned your bleeding feet the other way,
And we give thanks to you who chose for us.
So let us look with wonder on the swan,
The gift of God, the holy light of Christ,
Resplendent in his shining sinlessness.
The purity of Heaven is your gift.

Let us receive it now in thankfulness,
For your release. Your free, unfettered wings
Remind us that your freedom is our own,
Remind us that our freedom is of God.

I walk in stillness. Where my rest is set
Is Heaven. And the silence of the stars
Sings in a soundless circle. For the song
Of Heaven is past hearing, and ascends
Beyond the tiny range the ear can catch,
And soars into a spaceless magnitude
Where sound and silence meet in unity.
Holy am I, who brings my Father's Name
With me and who abides in Him, although
I seem to walk alone. Look carefully,
And you may catch a glimpse of Him who stands
Beside me. And I lean on Him in sure
Unswerving confidence. It was not thus
Before, for I was bitterly afraid
To take the Help of Heaven for my own.
Yet Heaven never failed, and only I
Stayed comfortless, while all of Heaven's gifts
Poured out before me. Now the arms of Christ
Are all I have and all my treasure is.
Now I have ceased to question. Now I come
From chaos to the stillness of my home.

THE GIFT

You are a blessing. You have come to me
Because He asked you to. And you have come
To speak to me about Him, so that He
Could show me through your voice the pathway home.

I had indeed been lost until He came.
Perhaps you did not know the gift you brought.
Yet what is one will always be the same,
And you will surely learn as you have taught.

You came because He asked, but did not know
He spoke to you of Him. His Voice came through
With crystal clarity. You came to show
The gift you brought to me is given you.

Your life is like a jewel in the crown,
The glowing light that Jesus promised me
When my own little light is laid aside.
Except your light is there my crown would be
A thing of time, to end as all things must,
Without an echo in eternity.

When comets pass they leave a path of light
Behind their going. It is this the sky
Remembers afterwards. We speak of Him
Who came in glory and Who seemed to die.
Yet in our light He lives again, and we
Must trail His shining likeness going by.

You are the light that stays behind a while
To bring His stillness and His peace to all
Who seek for Him in sorrow. In His Name
You will remain to answer to their call;
To sing to sleepless children and to raise
To His unfailing patience those who fall.

He waits for me as I will wait for you,
Standing with Him. In your unclouded sight
The world will vanish. Now He leans to you
And lifts you to your home. Behold how bright
The crown He has for you. Come now, my child,
And disappear with me into His light.

No one can know just what his part will mean
When God from little lights completes a star
From what we give to Him. Each is unseen
Until the other parts from near and far
Are joined by Him into a form that He
Can use to light the darkness. In His Hand
The stars are born, to shine upon the sea
And to enchant all things upon the land
And raise them Heavenward. Perhaps your gift
Is set upon a star tip, or perhaps
It shimmers at the center point, to lift
A heart from sadness. Or perhaps it caps
A silver star-side. Do not then forget
In what we value little God may see
A new-born star, unknown to us as yet
Who cannot look on glory still to be.

No one can rob infinity. For when
Something is taken, angels join their wings
And close the space so rapidly it seems
To be illusion; unoccurred, undone.

No one can take away from everything.
Its very wholeness is a guarantee
It is complete forever. There can be
No loss left unrestored before it comes.

No one can lessen love. It is itself
The Great Restorer. It can but return
All that is taken to itself. It knows
No loss, no limit and no lessening.

Heaven can only give. This is the sign
That losing is impossible. It seemed
That it was gone. Yet angels quickly came
And promised they would bring it back to you.

ANNIVERSARY

A year is short. Yet given unto Me
It lasts forever. Every minute is
Encased in silver; every hour in gold.
The months are splashed with stars, and they become
A diadem the angels will preserve
In shining brightness as your gift to Me.

It gains in glory every day it waits
For your returning. And the love in which
You gave it waits as well. My gratitude
Shines on its star points, polished carefully
By angels' wings, and kept immaculate
Against the time I give it back to you.

A Child, a Man and then a Spirit, come
In all Your loveliness. Unless You shine
Upon my life, it is a loss to You,
And what is loss to You is also mine.

I cannot calculate why I am here
Except for this: I know that I have come
To seek You here and find You. In Your life
You show the way to my eternal home.

A child, a man and then a spirit. So
I follow in the way You show to me
That I may come at last to be like You.
What but Your likeness would I want to be?

There is a silence where You speak to me
And give me words of love to say for You
To those You send to me. And I am blessed
Because in them I see You shining through.

There is no gratitude that I can give
For such a gift. The light around Your head
Must speak for me, for I am dumb beside
Your gentle hand with which my soul is led.

I take Your gift in holy hands, for You
Have blessed them with Your own. Come, brothers, see
How like to Christ am I, and I to you
Whom He has blessed and holds as one with me.

A perfect picture of what I can be
You show to me, that I might help renew
Your brothers' failing sight. As they look up
Let them not look on me, but only You.

Peace is a woman, mother to the world,
Whom God has sent to lay a gentle hand
Across a thousand children's fevered brows.
In its cool certainty there is no fear,
And from her breasts there comes a quietness
For them to lean against and to be still.

She brings a message to their frightened hearts
From Him Who sent her. Listen now to her
Who is your mother in your Father's Name:
"Do not attend the voices of the world.
Do not attempt to crucify again
My first-born Son, and brother still to you."

Heaven is in her eyes, because she looked
Upon this Son who was the first. And now
She looks to you to find him once again.
Do not deny the mother of the world
The only thing she ever wants to see,
For it is all you ever want to find.

BIRTHDAY

You neither come nor go. For even here
Your star is fixed within a little range
That holds its brightness still, without a change,
Until a brighter light starts to appear.

Fixed stars are guideposts to the earthly goal,
Pointing out pathways, avenues of hope,
And pitfalls of despair. Their little scope
Is merged into the grandeur of the Whole.

They do not vanish as the sun appears,
But add their little shining to the sum
Of promise of return. They seem to come
As resting-points against a world of fears.

Only your little light was born today,
Helping in darkness, to await the sun
And be enveloped in the Risen One
When you have done His will along the way.

NAME DAY

We celebrate a dream today; a dream
Of a beginning where no starting is,
Of shift and change and numbering of years,
As if we go to an appointed end.

Today we try to put a name upon
What has no name that it is given us
To name at all. What we can celebrate
Is only the illusion of a name.

This day is timeless. It was never born,
Nor will it end. There is no night to come,
No time in which the daylight disappears,
No turning back nor going on again.

Let us not celebrate what never was,
Nor think so little of the Son of God
That we imagine he was born today
And lost the Name that God has given him.

Let us choose rather that we see in him
The sweet reflection of his Father's love,
The sinlessness the Holy Spirit sees,
The help his holy brother looks upon.

The Holy Trinity shines over him,
The Father's love, the Holy Spirit's care,
The Son's completion, all are joined in one
Who shares eternity along with Them.

Therefore in quiet let us turn away
From days and hours; little names we give
To what we see but do not understand.
Hallowed your Name, for God created you.

The glory train goes riding by,
        Hallelujah!
A golden streaking in the sky,
A gleam and whistling rising high,
Above all souls that thought to die,
        Hallelujah!

Do not look up or you might see
An angel standing by the tree,
And see the halo round His head
And scream because you think you're dead.

The glory train will come at last,
        Hallelujah!
With crucifixion as a mast,
A blur of lightnin' ripping past
All things you love that will not last,
        Hallelujah!

Close up your ears or you might hear
The trumpet of the Charioteer,
And feel your heart's song miss a beat
To see His arrow at your feet.

Slow down the glory train for me,
        Hallelujah!
I see my Brother there and He
Is holding out a golden key
To raise my eyes that I might see,
        Hallelujah!

Come down, my Brother, come for me.
What fear has made I would not see.
The door is open. Where You stand
Is holy ground and Heavenland.

I did not understand the song,
        Hallelujah!
I thought to die but now I long
Only to join the risen throng
That rides the stars with You along,
        Hallelujah!

There is no death, and life rides by
Until You stop to raise us high
And touch our eyes and ears, so we
Long deaf and blind, can hear and see,
        Hallelujah!

I came to you.
I saw your tears and knew
That you were ready. You had asked Me in
The instant that you understood that sin
Is an illusion. You were poor indeed.
I saw your grasping hands and watched them bleed
From golden nails; a heavy jewelled crown
Around your head, as sacred as My Own.

I needed you
As much. Yet till you grew
In understanding, I could only wait
In silent patience beyond Heaven's gate.
My Father's house stood empty. For as we
Are part of Him, so are you part of Me.
We enter in together. We are one.
And so I finish what I had begun.

Love does not crucify. It only saves.
God's Son cannot be hurt. Let him not think
That he is slave to time or punishment.
Created out of Love, his shining head
And loving heart can only save the world.
Who but its maker can redeem it? What
Except the Word of truth can liberate
Whom he imprisons? Let him be Himself,
And not one star can lose a single gleam,
Or flicker in uncertain galaxy
Without a purpose and without a cause.
No blade of grass but rises perfectly
From earth toward Heaven. And no sin appears
To hold in shadows whom all Heaven loves.
God does not crucify. He merely is.

Who stands beside a cross is all alone,
For sorrow such as this cannot be shared.
A pit is cut into the solid rock
Between the world and her. No bridge, no hand
Can reach across to comfort. Silently
She stands, without the bitter help of tears,
For tears were made for ordinary grief
Which long ago had come and been surpassed.

Here time is reckoned differently. A month
Is held in every instant, and the years
Pass by in grim procession in the space
That others call an hour. Yet for her
They reach into eternity. She stands
Upon the edge of eons without hope.
Here is forever. Here is timelessness.
Who could believe the time of dying ends?

DEDICATION FOR AN ALTAR

Temples are where God's holy altars are,
And He has placed an altar in each Son
Whom He created. Let us worship here
In thankfulness that what He gives to one
He gives to all, and never takes away.
For what He wills has been forever done.

Temples are where a brother comes to pray
And rest a while. Whoever he may be,
He brings with him a lighted lamp to show
My Savior's face is there for me to see
Upon the altar, and remember God.
My brother, come and worship here with me.

Silence and nothing more. There is no sound
And nothing to be seen. No fingers still
Grasp at the world. All prayers have been forgot,
For there is nothing now that can be asked.

The Voice for God no longer speaks. There is
No need remaining. There was once a time,
Now unremembered, when there was a world.
A Word is spoken, and the world is done.

Christ passes no one by. By this you know
He is God's Son. You recognize His touch
In universal gentleness. His Love
Extends to everyone. His eyes behold
The Love of God in everything He sees.
No words but those His Father's Voice dictates
Can reach His ears. His hands forever hold
His brothers', and His arms remain outstretched
In holy welcome. Would you look on Him,
And hear Him calling you this Christmas day?

Behold, He offers you His eyes to see,
His ears to listen to His Father's Voice,
His hands to hold His brothers', and His arms
To reach to Him as He would reach to you.
You are as like to Him as He to God,
And you to God because you are like Him.
All that He offers you is but your own.
Accept His gifts to you this Christmas day,
That you who are as God created you,
May come to recognize the Christ in you.

There was an instant long ago when God
Proclaimed His Word, and all the world was still
To hear and answer. Yet it could not hear
Nor answer. When the holy Christ was born
He came alone, with but His Father's Word
To hear and answer Him. And yet His Voice
Remains to bless the world along with me
Who would remember that His Word is mine.

Christmas is holy only if you come
In silence to the manger, to behold
Your holiness made visible to you.
Your gifts are but your open hands, made clean
Of grasping. Nothing else you lay before
The newly-born except your doubts and fears,
Your pale illusions and your sickly pride,
Your hidden venom and your little love,
Your meager treasures and unfaithfulness
To all the gifts that God has given you.
Here at the altar lay all this aside
To let the door to Heaven open wide
And hear the angels sing of peace on earth,
For Christmas is the time of your rebirth.

Christ is not born but neither does He die,
And yet He is reborn in everyone.
The rising and the birth are one in Him,
For it is in the advent of God's Son
The light of resurrection is begun.

Heaven needs no nativity. And yet
The Son of Heaven needs the world to be
His birthplace, for the world is overcome
Because a Child is born. And it is He
Who brings God's promise of eternity.

It is His birth that ends the dream of death,
For in Him death is brought to life. Behold
The earth made new and shining in the hope
Of love and pardon. Now God's Arms enfold
The hearts that shivered in the winter's cold.

There is an altar that I seek. For there
And only there can certain peace be found.
The light of holiness shines white upon
Its cooling stillness wreathed with lilies round.
Here is the place where those who thought that death
Was lord of life must come, to learn of One
Who seemed to die, that life is lord of death.
Beside the lilies sickly dreams are gone,
And stillness spreads a blanket over all
Who seemed to know no rest and find no peace,
To bring the quiet and the dreamless sleep
In which their dreaming will forever cease.
Here we awake, my brothers and myself,
For all of us come here to find the way
To waken from the dream of sin the world
Was made to represent. We come to lay
Our guilt beside the altar and step back,
Putting illusions and mistakes aside,
And learn before an empty tomb to see,
He is not dead Who here was crucified.

You think Him dead Who rose again for you,
And so you cannot see the shining light
In which you are delivered. Come, My child,
And judge Him not. He is not dead. So bright
His radiance that nothing still remains
Obscured from Heaven in the doubt of night.

So still the birth you did not understand
Who came to you. Before your frightened eyes
The Lord of light and life appears to fail
His promises of Heaven's grace, and dies
Forever on a cross. Nor can you see
The Child of hope Who in a manger lies.

The wise are silent. Stand you by a while
And let the wise men show you what they see
That came of you from stillness and from peace
Which rest in you, but speak to them of Me.
And then be comforted. The living Lord
Has come again where He has willed to be.

Wait now for morning. In the silence hear
The winged whispering that hails the Son
In quiet certainty and lovely calm
Whom death released to life. He is the One
For Whom you wait. Then look again on Him,
And join His benediction, "It is done."

He held you in His arms as He arose,
And death was overcome. Yet on the hill
Of dying you had fixed your eyes, it seemed

As if forever. Now you wait until
You look beyond the end you thought you saw,
And see the Child Who is your first-born still.

Think of this Child Who comes again. He is
The Son Who seemed to die. He offers you
The motherhood the shadow of a cross
Appeared to take away. Yet round it grew
The lilies of rebirth. Accept again
The deathless One, the holy Son you knew.

See not an ending where beginning is,
Nor dark in sunlight. You who came to mourn,
Remember now the ancient song of birth,
And lay aside the signs of grieving worn
By childless mothers. Lift your heart to Him,
For once again to you a Child is born.

THE SECOND EASTER

A bird sang first and then the Lord arose.
He could not disappoint a little part
Of God's creation, which had held its faith
Unwavering within its tiny heart.

Disciples doubted, women wept, and those
Who had been faithful had betrayed the trust
Of Him Whose promise had been one of life,
And yet Who seemed to fall away to dust.

What is the resurrection but the end
Of little frightened cries; the answerings
Of doubts unspoken and the loss of hope
That flutters helplessly on broken wings.

Yet to all these it comes unrecognized,
For those who grieve cannot behold the light
Through veils of sorrow. They forget the Word
That promised to redeem their failing sight.

Where there is faith the resurrection comes
In full awareness, blazing like the sun
That shines past darkness, as a Voice calls out,
"It is not over. It has just begun."

A song of faith, and then the Lord of life
Comes forth in gratitude for trust held fast
By those who still remembered that He said,
"I will return." And He has come at last.

The dead are dead. They do not rise again.
And yet I see in You a look I knew
In One so recently destroyed and laid
Away to wither on a slab of stone.

I almost could believe – but I have seen
Your blue and bloodless hands and broken feet,
The way You crumpled when they took You down.
This is a stranger, and I know Him not.

The road is long. I will not lift my eyes,
For fear has gripped my heart, and fear I know –
The shield that keeps me safe from rising hope;
The friend that keeps You stranger still to me.

Why should You walk with me along the road,
An unknown whom I almost think I fear
Because You seem like someone in a dream
Of deathlessness, when death alone is real?

Do not disturb me now. I am content
With death, for grief is kinder now than hope.
While there was hope I suffered. Now I go
In certainty, for death has surely come.

Do not disturb the ending. What is done
Is done forever. Neither hope nor tears
Can touch finality. Do not arouse
The dead. Come, Stranger, let us say "Amen."

You said You would return, and I believed
Too long already. Now my eyes are sealed
Against the slender thread of hope that cuts
Into my calm despair. O let me go!

Your Word surrounds You like a golden light,
And I can scarcely see the road we walk
Because my eyes are veiled. Disturb me not,
I beg of You. I would not see You now.

Must I remember now? And yet the light
Seems even brighter, and the road becomes
A sudden splash of sunlight. Who are You
Who dares to enter into fear and death?

Your Voice reminds me of an ancient song
My lips begin to sing, although I hoped
It was forgotten. Now I hear again
A Word I thought had been forever dead,

As You had died. I cannot keep my eyes
From looking up. Perhaps I did not see
The things I thought. Perhaps this light has come
To heal my eyes and let them see again.

Lord, did You really keep Your lovely Word?
Was I mistaken? Did You rise again?
And was it I who failed, instead of You?
Are You returned to save me from the dead?

Dear Stranger, let me recognize Your face,
And all my doubts are answered. They are dead
If You are living. Let me see again,
And hope will be transformed to certainty.

The dead are dead, but they do rise again.
Let me remember only that. It was
The rest that was the dream. The light has come.
My eyes are opening to look on You.

There is no death. But there is quietness
Beyond the reaches of the world; a peace
Which only life can give. It is the life
That is the gift of God. All conflicts cease
Within this life. It beats in harmony
With all creation, beyond any sound
The world can hear. It sings a different song,
And where it reaches, there is holy ground.

There is no death. Whom God created whole
Is whole forever. Who can crucify
Eternal life? And who can bring to dust
Whom God has willed immortal? Can he die
Who rises past the universe, to rest
At one with his Creator? So are we
Ensured to life. There is no death because
God's Son belongs to Immortality.

This is a day of joy. Today the world
Lays down its dreams beside a cross that was
Itself a dream. Behold the dream of death
And waken, seeing that it had no cause,
And so did not exist. What never was
Can not be now. Today we pass it by,
For this the purpose of this day should be:
What is made whole is whole, and cannot die.

Do not confuse the cross with sacrifice,
Nor death with life. The Will of God is one,
And knows no differences nor opposites.

In love it has created but one Son,
In whom the whole creation still remains.
How can his name be changed who bears the Name
His Father called as His? He does not change,
Because his will forever is the same.

What does he yearn for but his Father's house?
Had he a different will his death might be
Reality. But when he reconciled
What never had an opposite, then he
Could never die. His life is not his own,
Being of God. This day arise and come
With Me. For there is life. It is God's Will.
Today shall you be with Me in our home.

The door is solid. Ancient keys are gone.
The rusted hinge stands firm. The bolt is shut,
And spiders' castles shimmer in the gleam
Of tired moonlight. Everything seems put
In place forever, and decay has come
To wage a ceaseless war against the hope
Of sunlight. What was once a window stands
Like blackness in the dark. My fingers grope
Along the walls and bleed on granite thorns.
I would not hear You knock. The air is thin,
And whistles through the small remaining gap
Upon the dark that lets the moon's edge in.

I fell so long ago I could not come
To let You enter, even if I heard
You knock against the door. I could not reach
The crumbling handle, nor could speak the word
Of welcome that would ask You enter and
Abide with me. Your light would shock my eyes
Long used to darkness, and to dim effects
That shift like shadows round where someone dies,
And wander back and forth and forth and back
Till light becomes unwanted. Did You say
That You would never leave me till the end?
Time has no meaning now.

Was it a day,
A month, a year, – eternity, – since You
Promised to come? You said You would redeem
The world. Yet I can only see a cross.
The resurrection seems to be a dream.

I did not die. In rising up I did
But stay the same. Eternity had come
To claim its own from the embrace of time
And bitter kiss of death. I but came home
After a journey so diminutive
That Heaven never noticed it began
Nor ended. Unencumbered, changelessly,
The Christ united with the Son of man,
And what belonged to God returned to Him.
Think not the Holy Spirit waits for death
To offer you the gifts God gave to Him,
Or Heaven rests upon a failing breath.

I did not die. Appearances of hate
Enveloped Me. Illusions veiled My eyes
And stopped My heart. Earth's dream closed over Me,
And that was all. The Son of God must rise
Above all dreams of fear. Would God allow
The Son who is like Him to separate
From life that is Himself? His Comforter
Came down to lift Me up within His great
And silent wings. The peace of God unbound
My hands and feet. For who can stop the Heart
Of God Himself, or veil the eyes that watch
His Son in mercy, or make Him depart
From what is but Himself?

I did not die.
The dream of sacrifice but died for Me.
Seek not illusions now. Be still and stop
The worshipping of death. Look up and see
My feet upon the shining mountain top.

You came but for a while. When Jesus called
You were content to go. For who would stay
To watch the dreary cycle of the nights
Turn coldly gray with each return of day?

This world was not your home. Would God allow
His child to wander long without a home
Which He Himself makes bright? Your tired eyes
Closed gratefully when He at last said, "Come."

You have forgot all this. All thoughts that hurt,
All sorrow, all regret, have ceased to be
In your remembrance. He Who called to you
Has loosened all your chains and set you free.

Because I love you I would have you go.
Because I love Him I can scarcely weep.
Because He loves you glory goes with you,
And in that glory you but seem to sleep.

He came in mercy. Let me give Him thanks
You stayed with us until you saw Him smile
And tell you it is finished. He will come
For me that way in just a little while.

It is for this I wait, in certainty
That He Who made the stars will not forget.
I will be glad to see Him smile at me,
Or if He choose, to wait a little yet.

The Gifts of God

The Dream of Fear

Fear is the one emotion of the world. Its forms are many–call them what you will – but it is one in content. Never far, even in form, from what its purpose is, never with power to escape its cause, and never but a counterfeit of joy, it rests uncertainly upon a bed of lies. Here it was born and sheltered by its seeming comfort. Here it will remain where it was born, and where its end will come. For here is nothingness, where neither birth nor death is real, nor any form in the misshapen mind that spawned its seeming life has any meaning in the Mind of God.

If you were certain – wholly sure and with consistent grasp of what the world can give – fear would be laid aside as easily as joy and peace unite on love's behalf. But first there must be certainty that there can be no love where fear exists, and that the world will never give a gift which is not made of fear, concealed perhaps, but which is surely present somewhere in the gift. Accept it not, and you will understand a gift far greater has been given you.

Let not the world deceive you. It was made to be deception. Yet its snares can be so easily escaped a little child can walk through safely, and without a care that would arrest its progress. Dreams are dreams, and every one is equally untrue. This is the only lesson to be learned. Yet will fear linger until every one is recognized as nothingness, and seen exactly as it is and nothing more. There is no person, thing or circumstance that you can value as your own without the "gift" of fear arising in your heart. For you have seen them all as they are not, and love for them has fled as if from you. And you will think that God has ceased to care for you who have betrayed the Son He loves, and chosen fear and guilt in place of Him.

Does God deceive or does the world? For it is sure that one must lie. There is no point at which their thoughts agree, their gifts unite in kind or purpose. What you take from one the other will obscure. There is no hope of compromise in this. Nor can there be a shifting of the mind between the two without the fear that every dream must bring. How fearful it must be to see yourself a maker of reality and truth, the lord of destiny and time's domain, and arbiter appointed for the world.

Dreams never change. Remember only this, but do not let it slip away at times and let yourself give way to fear again. Deny the dream but do not fail the truth, for only what is true will never fail. All else deceives. All else will terrify, and even when it seems to please the most it brings with it a heavy cost of pain. Be free of suffering now. There is no cost for any gift that comes to you from God. His way is certain, for His gifts remain forever as He gave them. Do not think that fear can enter where His gifts abide. But do not think gifts can be received where fear has entered, and has touched your sight with gross distortions that the world thinks real.

There are no scraps of dreams. Each one contains the whole of fear, the opposite of love, the hell that hides the memory of God, the crucifixion of His holy Son. Therefore, be vigilant against them all, for in their single purpose they are one, and hell is total. It can seem to take forever for this lesson to be learned, and yet it need not be. I come to speak in time of timelessness. Have you not learned the pain of dreaming yet? There is no need to hug it to your heart, and to forget the dreadful cost of salvaging despair and building up deceptions once again.

The tiniest of dreams, the smallest wish for values of the world is large enough to stand between you and the sweet release that God would offer you. He cannot choose to change His Son, nor make your mind accept the perfect freedom He has given you. Yet it is certain you will turn to Him and suddenly remember. But be sure of this and do not let it slip away: What God has joined is one. And one as well is everything that fear has made to be the great deceiver and the substitute for God's creation. You can choose but one, and which you choose is total. Everything the world can offer promises some joy that it will never give. And everything that God has promised you will never fail in anything. No need will be unmet, no hurt unhealed, no sorrow kept unchanged, no darkness undispelled. The smallest pain will vanish suddenly before His gifts. An unremembered world will leave no trace behind its going, when God's gifts have been accepted as the only things you want.

"Choose once again" is still your only hope. Darkness cannot conceal the gifts of God unless you want it so. In peace I come, and urge you now to make an end to time and step into eternity with me. There will not be a change that eyes can see, nor will you disappear from things of time. But you will hold my hand as you return because we come together. Now the hosts of Heaven come with us, to sweep away all vestiges of dreams and every thought that rests on nothingness. How dear are you to God, Who asks but that you walk with me and bring His light into a sickened world which fear has drained of love and life and hope.

Surely you will not fail to hear my call, for I have never failed to hear your cries of pain and grief, and I have come to save and to redeem the world at last from fear. It never was, nor is, nor yet will be what you imagine. Let me see for you, and judge for you what you would look upon. When you have seen with me but once, you would no longer value any fearful thing at cost of glory and the peace of God.

This is my offering: A quiet world, with gentle ordering and kindly thought, alive with hope and radiant in joy, without the smallest bitterness of fear upon its loveliness. Accept this now, for I have waited long to give this gift to you. I offer it in place of fear and all the "gifts" that fear has given you. Can you choose otherwise, when all the world is standing breathless, waiting on your choice? Come now to me and we will go to God. There is no way that we can go alone. But when we come together there can be no way in which the Word of God can fail. For His the Word that makes us one in Him, and mine the Voice that speaks this Word to you.

The Two Gifts

How can you be delivered from all gifts the world has offered you? How can you change these little, cruel offerings for those that Heaven gives and God would have you keep? Open your hands, and give all things to me that you have held against your holiness and kept as slander on the Son of God. Practice with every one you recognize as what it is. Give me these worthless things the instant that you see them through my eyes and understand their cost. Then give away these bitter dreams as you perceive them now to be but that, and nothing more than that.

I take them from you gladly, laying them beside the gifts of God that He has placed upon the altar to His Son. And these I give to you to take the place of those you give to me in mercy on yourself. These are the gifts I ask, and only these. For as you lay them by you, reach to me, and I can come as savior then to you. The gifts of God are in my hands, to give to anyone who would exchange the world for Heaven. You need only call my name and ask me to accept the gift of pain from willing hands that would be laid in mine, with thorns laid down and nails long thrown away as one by one the sorry gifts of earth are joyously relinquished. In my hands is everything you want and need and hoped to find among the shabby toys of earth. I take them all from you and they are gone. And shining in the place where once they stood there is a gateway to another world through which we enter in the Name of God.

Father, we thank You for these gifts that we have found together. Here we are redeemed. For it is here we joined, and from this place of holy joining we will come to You because we recognize the gifts You gave and would have nothing else. Each hand that finds its way to mine will take Your gifts from me, and as we look together on the place whereon I laid your worthless gifts for you, we will see nothing but the gifts of God reflected in the shining round our heads.

Holy are we who know our holiness, for it is You Who shine Your light on us, and we are thankful, in Your ancient Name, that You have not forgotten. What we thought we made of You has merely disappeared, and with its going are the images we made of Your creation gone as well. And it is finished. For we now commend into Your Hands the spirit of Your Son who seemed to lose his way a little while but never left the safety of Your Love. The gifts of fear, the dream of death, are done. And we give thanks. And we give thanks, Amen.

The Ending of the Dream

Illusions are made as substitutes for truth, for which no substitutes are possible. Creator separate from creation was the first illusion, where all gifts of fear were born. For now creation could not be like its Creator, Who could never leave what He Himself created part of Him. Now must there be a substitute for love, which cannot have an opposite in truth and, being all, can have no substitute.

So fear was made, and with it came the need for gifts to lend the substance to a dream in which there is no substance. Now the dream seems to have value, for its offerings appear as hope and strength and even love, if only for an instant. They content the frightened dreamer for a little while, and let him not remember the first dream which gifts of fear but offer him again. The seeming solace of illusions' gifts are now his armor, and the sword he holds to save himself from waking. For before he could awaken, he would first be forced to call to mind the first dream once again.

It is not God Who asks a price of him, but having drawn a veil across the truth, he now must let the veil be drawn away so that its lack of substance can be seen. No one would hesitate to leave a dream of shock and terror, merciless decay and sickening contortions, with despair always in sight and death not far behind, if he believed that it *were* but a dream. Yet if he thinks that he must first go through a greater terror still, he must see hope in what will now appear the "better" dream.

And now he seeks within his dream to find what gifts it may contain. What can you get within its shadows? Who can save you now by giving you the love you threw away? What can you learn to do to make yourself a master over others? What is there that is your special gift within the dream? Find these and do not waken from the dream, for it can give you what you think you lack. But if you waken, all its gifts will go, your armor and your sword will disappear, and vultures, always circling overhead, will claim you as their lawful prey at last.

O children of the Father you forgot, you have not put your idols in His place, nor made Him give the gifts of fear you made. Let me be Savior from illusions. Truth may be concealed from you by evil dreams, but it is only from the dreams that you have need from saving. Truth is still untouched by your deceptions. Yet you cannot go past that first dream without a

Savior's hand in yours. Each gift of fear would hold you back unless you let me lift it from your mind by showing you that it is but a dream within a larger dream of hopelessness in which there *is* no hope. Take not its gifts, for they condemn you to a lasting hell which will endure when all the seeming joy the gifts appeared to give have passed away.

Do not be tempted. Do not fall away into the shadows and a deeper sleep in which the waking seems to be the dream. Help me give you salvation. Let us share the strength of Christ and look upon the dream in which illusions started, and which serve to keep their birthplace secret and apart from the illumination of the truth. Come unto me. There is no need to dream of an escape from dreaming. It will fail. For if the dream were real, escape would be impossible and there would be no hope *except* illusions. Do not yield to this. It is not so. For I am not a dream that comes in mockery. Salvation needs your help as well as mine. Do not forget you do not answer for yourself alone.

My call to you is that you offer help from all the dreams the holy Son of God imagines, from the time that first of dreams was given false reality until all dreaming ends forever. Could a gift be holier than this? And could the need within a world of dreams be more acute or more compelling? Give me help in this, and not one gift the world may seek to give, nor one illusion held against the truth, can bind you longer. Time can have no sway upon you, nor can any laws of earth have power over you. Your hands will heal and give the gifts that you accept of me.

How joyful and how holy is our way when death has no dominion, and the dream of separation, agony and loss has been dispelled forever. Do not think that anything the gifts of fear hold out is worth an instant's hesitation, when the gate of Heaven stands before you and the Christ of God is waiting your return. Be still and hear Him, for His call to you could not be more insistent nor more dear, for it is but the call of Love itself, which will not cease to speak of God to you. You have forgot. But He is faithful still, because He is so like His Father He remembers Him forever in His Love. And He cannot forget creation is inseparable from Creator, so He understands that you are part of God and of the Son created like Himself.

How dear are you, a part of Christ in Whom is every gift of God forever laid, without which is He incomplete, Who is completion of His Father. Can a dream destroy a truth so holy and so pure that it encompasses all truth, and leaves nothing beyond itself? Can you betray a love so perfect that its gifts become itself in oneness, and this single gift is all there is to give and to receive? O come and let creation be again all that it always was and still will be forever and forever. Let the dream of time be given its appointed end, and let God's Son have mercy on himself.

There is a silence covering the world that was an ancient dream so long ago no one remembers now. Its time is done, and in the little space it seemed to own is nothingness. The dream has gone, and all its dreams of gifts have disappeared as well. The first dream has been seen and understood for merely an illusion of the fear on which the world was based. Beyond the dream, reaching to everything, embracing all, creation and Creator still remain in perfect harmony and perfect love. This is beyond the gate at which we stand. And shall we stay to wait upon a dream?

Your holiness is mine, and mine is God's. Here is His gift, complete and undefiled. It is Himself He gives, and it is this that is the truth in you. How beautiful are you who stand beside me at the gate, and call with me that everyone may come and step aside from time. Put out your hand to touch eternity and disappear into its perfect rest. Here is the peace that God intended for the Son He loves. Enter with me and let its quietness cover the earth forever. It is done. Father, your Voice has called us home at last: Gone is the dream. Awake, My child, in love.

Our Gift to God

There is no gift of faith that God does not accept with gratitude. He loves His Son. And as He gives His gifts to him, so is He grateful for the gifts His Son gives Him. Gratitude is the song of Heaven's gift, the single harmony that is sung by all creation at one with its Creator. For gratitude is love expressed in joining; the necessary precondition for extension and the prerequisite for peace. And who can be in conflict and love God?

We have discussed the gifts of God to you. Now we must also speak of those that you can give to Him. For these complete His giving, as it is His to you that make you whole. Giving is joy and holiness and healing. Here is your answer to the world, and God's as well. For here it is you join with Him, His likeness being yours in this alone.

How can you give to Him Who has no lack, no emptiness, no need, no unlit place which needs a light that you can offer Him? He saves your gifts for you. He does not know of giving and receiving. What is love, or comes from love, or offers love a gift, is one to Him because it is of Him. To Him and from Him are not different to One Who has no opposite. For love is all there is and everything there is. A gift to love is given everyone, not lessening the giver, nor in truth adding to the receiver. More than love there cannot be. But this a gift becomes if it is truly given and received by both to both who know that they are one: A key to silence and the peace of God, a glad acknowledgment of love of Christ, a greeting to the Holy Spirit's help, an invitation that He enter in and lift the Son of God unto Himself.

What more would God hold dearer, then, than this? These are His gifts as much as they are yours, for in them giver and receiver join. A gift is holy only when there is no sense at all of who will gain thereby, and not a shadow of a thought of loss. It is not easy in the world to know what giving means, and how to give a gift that God and all creation will accept as shining outward from a thankful heart and inward to the altar of its God.

God gives the grace to give as He must give, for He must give the only way He knows, and what He knows is everything He is. Christ gives as He does, being like Himself. And nothing stands outside the gifts They give, for every gift is all-encompassing and lifts the universe into Their Arms.

Yet what of you who seem to be on earth, and do not understand what giving is because you have forgotten what love means? What gifts are there that you can give to God? My brother, there are many calls to you from those who lost their way and need your help in finding it again. It seems to you that you are helping them if you respond to what they ask and what you think they need. Yet it is always God Who calls to you, and he who asks your help is but yourself. Who is the giver and receiver then? Who asks the gift and who is given it?

This is the only lesson that the world must teach in giving. It is not the one the world was made to teach. And yet it is the one the Holy Spirit sees in it, and so it is the only one it has. Forget the other devastating ways the gifts of earth are given and received. Forget the cost, the thoughts of loss and gain, the bargaining, the counting of the score, the world associates with every gift it gives in strict accordance with its laws. The money-changers of the marketplace have been your teachers. Now they need a gift they could not give. Be savior now to them because you have another Teacher now.

Count not the cost of giving. There is none. Your teachers

have deceived. But do not think that their mistakes were not your own as well. To all who do not understand the gifts of God and Christ are one, be yours the voice that echoes what the Voice for God would say:

"Save Me, My brother, as you save yourself,
And let Me give to God your gifts for you
Because His altar waits for them in love,
And He is asking that We place them there."

There is no love but God's; no gift but His. We but return His Own unto Himself. But as we do, He comes to call His Son from the far country where he threw away the memory of all his Father's gifts, and ask him to return again to Him.

Child of Eternal Love, what gift is there your Father wants of you except yourself? And what is there that you would rather give, for what is there that you would rather have? You have forgotten Who you really are. What but that memory is dear to you? What trifling gifts made out of sickly fear and evil dreams of suffering and death can be the substitute you really want for the rememberance of Christ in you? In the far country you were lost indeed, but you were not forgotten. Hear the call of love to love, by love, in love to you, and rise with love beside you to return the gift of love that God has given you, and you have given Him in gratitude.

Do not forget the Source of what you are, and do not think He has forgotten you. Love does not waver, and does not forget the gift it gives that it would have you keep. Return them, then, for it is dark indeed in the far country, where God's memory has seemed to disappear. Yet Christ has come wherever you have gone. For you are His, and being His you are His Father's, too. He brings with Him the gifts His Father gave, and giving them to you He teaches you how to return them in the way He gives. Light knows no limit; love no lessening. Return, My child, to Me. For Christ is He Who is My Son and you are one with Him. You are My gift, for you are one with Me.

The Father's Love

There is a secret place in everyone in which God's gifts are laid, and his to Him. It is not secret to the eyes of Christ Who sees it plainly and unceasingly. Yet it is hidden to the body's eyes, and to those still invested in the world and caring for the petty gifts it gives, esteeming them and thinking they are real. Illusions' gifts will hide the secret place where God is clear as day, and Christ with Him. O let this not be secret to the world so full of sorrow and so racked with pain. You could relieve its grief and heal its pain, and let the peace of God envelop it as does a mother rock a tired child until it sighs and slips away to rest.

Rest could be yours because of what God is. He loves you as a mother loves her child; her only one, the only love she has, her all-in-all, extension of herself, as much a part of her as breath itself. He loves you as a brother loves his own; born of one father, still as one in him, and bonded with a seal that cannot break. He loves you as a lover loves his own; his chosen one, his joy, his very life, the one he seeks when she has gone away, and brings him peace again on her return. He loves you as a father loves his son, without whom would his self be incomplete, whose immortality completes his own, for in him is the chain of love complete – a golden circle that will never end, a song that will be sung throughout all time and afterwards, and always will remain the deathless sound of loving and of love.

O be at peace, beloved of the Lord! What is your life but gratitude to Him Who loves you with an everlasting Love? What is your purpose here but to recall into His loving Arms the Son He loves, who has forgotten Who his Father is? What is your only goal, your only hope, your only need, the only thing you want, but to allow the secret place of peace to burst upon the world in all its joy, and let the Voice within it speak of Him Whose love shines out and in and in-between, through all the darkened places to embrace all living things within its golden peace?

The night is dark but it will have an end. Be comforted with this: No one I send to help you reach the goal will fail to stand beside you till your kingdom is secure. The promises of God are given you. What could be surer? There is help indeed for one so near to Heaven. There is change in everything but this; whom He has called and who has answered Him as you have done can rest in peace upon His loving Arm, and trust His gratitude and thankful Heart to beat for yours when yours appears to fail.

Do not imagine He will leave His child who heard His Voice and listened to His Word. Remember this: The thanks of God are yours and will not leave you comfortless for long. You still are needed in the world, to hear His Voice and share His messages of love with those who call in sorrow. Could it be that you will fail to find Him, when His need for you becomes as great as yours for Him? You need not fear that you will suffer loss, nor that He will abandon you who gave His comfort to His Son. Receive the gift you gave to God and He would give to you.

Trust Him Whose Voice you heard, and do not think He does not hear your frightened voice that calls in whispered agony. You will be raised from terror to the shining peace of God. The way seems thorny and beset with grief, yet it is certain as the Love of God which cannot fail. It holds you up, and so you cannot fail because it shines in you. Faith will be yours because His faith in you is limitless. Do not despair of Him

Who loves you with an everlasting Love; Who knows your need and watches over you in everything with ceaseless vigilance.

Do not forget His thanks, and understand the gratitude of God goes far beyond all things the world can offer, for His Gifts will last forever in His Heart and ours. Be thankful for His Love and for His care, for in this world it has been given few to give a gift to God as you have done. Yet only few are needed. They suffice for all the rest, and they give thanks to you along with their Creator and with yours. He is not careless of the gifts He gives, nor are His promises in vain. Be sure a mother does not fail the son she loves, nor will a Father cast away His child.

You are My Son, and I do not forget the secret place in which I still abide, knowing you will remember. Come, My Son, open your heart and let Me shine on you, and on the world through you. You are My light and dwelling place. You speak for Me to those who have forgotten. Call them now to Me, My Son, remember now for all the world. I call in love, as you will answer Me, for this the only language that we know. Remember love, so near you cannot fail to touch its heart because it beats in you.

Do not forget. Do not forget, My child. Open the door before the hidden place, and let Me blaze upon a world made glad in sudden ecstasy. I come, I come. Behold Me. I am here for I am You; in Christ, for Christ, My Own beloved Son, the glory of the infinite, the joy of Heaven and the holy peace of earth, returned to Christ and from His hand to Me. Say now Amen, My Son, for it is done. The secret place is open now at last. Forget all things except My changeless Love. Forget all things except that I am here.

Appendix

I. Early Poems

The Singing Reed . . . March 12, 1971
Benediction . . . September 11, 1971
The Last Judgment . . . September 12, 1971
Christ's Vision . . . September 13, 1971
Our Daily Bread . . . September 13, 1971
The Holy Instant . . . September 15, 1971
The Holy Purpose . . . September 15, 1971
The Will of God . . . September 16, 1971
Safety . . . September 20, 1971
The Real World . . . September 16, 1971
The Holy Relationship . . . September 20, 1971
The Song of Peace . . . September 23, 1971
The Face of Christ . . . September 23, 1971
Alternatives . . . September 23, 1971
The Call of Christ . . . September 23, 1971
Thy Kingdom Come . . . September 23, 1971
Correction . . . September 23, 1971
Redemption . . . September 23, 1971
The Promise . . . September 29, 1971
The Little Things of God . . . September 29, 1971
The Circular Way . . . September 29, 1971
Quietness . . . September 29, 1971
Renunciation . . . September 30, 1971
Definition . . . September 30, 1971
Identity . . . September 30, 1971
God's Likeness . . . September 30, 1971
Heaven's Messengers . . . October 1, 1971
The Christ Thought . . . October 1, 1971
The Greeting . . . October 3, 1971
Christ's Need . . . October 4, 1971
The Final Vision . . . October 5, 1971
It Is Finished . . . October 4, 1971
The Mirrors of Christ . . . October 5, 1971

The Arch of Silence . . . October 10, 1971
The Inner Light . . . October 10, 1971
The Joining . . . October 10, 1971
Anger Is Done . . . October 10, 1971
The Certain Help . . . October 12, 1971
The Singing . . . October 12, 1971
The Recognition . . . October 12, 1971
Healing . . . October 12, 1971
Morning . . . October 20, 1971
The Eternal Safety . . . October 20, 1971
The Silent Way . . . October 20, 1971
The Mirror of Forgiveness . . . October 27, 1971
The Certain Way . . . October 27, 1971
The Sign . . . October 28, 1971
The Timeless Gifts . . . October 28, 1971
His Certainty . . . October 28, 1971
They Wait . . . October 28, 1971
Before We Ask . . . November 2, 1971
Our Common Goal . . . November 2, 1971
The Little Gift . . . November 3, 1971
Stillness . . . November 3, 1971
He Asks but This . . . November 8, 1971
Song to My Self . . . November 11, 1971
The Tiny Instant . . . November 11, 1971

II. Personal Poems

Bright Stranger . . . January 1, 1974
The Ancient Love . . . February 23, 1974
The Second Chance . . . December 27, 1973
Arise with Me . . . January 1, 1974
The Last Prayer . . . January 2, 1974
Come unto Me . . . February 23, 1974
Prayer for a House . . . March 2, 1974
The Wayside Cross . . . March 4, 1974

The Saving Gamble . . . April 11, 1974
Waiting . . . November 11, 1976
Love Song . . . January 8, 1977
The Resting Place . . . February 7, 1977
Deliverance . . . February 8, 1977

III. Later Poems

My Father's House . . . December 24, 1973
The End of Time . . . December 27, 1973
Conversion . . . December 25, 1973
Access . . . December 26, 1973
A Brother's Prayer . . . January 3, 1976
Transformation . . . April 9, 1974
The Quiet Dream . . . February 5, 1974
The Star Form . . . April 8, 1974
Long Darkness . . . January 26, 1974
The Greater Gift . . . January 10, 1974
The Comforter . . . January 1, 1974
The Risen Sun . . . February 11, 1974
Awake in Stillness . . . January 15, 1974
This Shining Instant . . . March 17, 1974
Brother Swan . . . January 3, 1977
The Soundless Song . . . March 17, 1974
The Gift . . . December 23, 1975
Continuity . . . May 6, 1977
With Thanks . . . August 24, 1975
Heaven's Gift . . . January 28, 1977
Anniversary . . . September 12, 1974
A Jesus Prayer . . . February 16, 1976
Mother of the World . . . February 23, 1974
Birthday . . . February 21, 1975
Name Day . . . February 21, 1978
The Glory Train . . . October 24, 1975
The Invitation . . . January 1, 1974

Amen . . . November 12, 1974
Stabat Mater . . . December 21, 1976
Dedication for an Altar . . . August 24, 1974
The Peace of God . . . November 12, 1974
The Gifts of Christmas . . . December 25, 1969
Nativity . . . December 24, 1973
The Holiness of Christmas . . . December 25, 1973
The Hope of Christmas . . . December 11, 1975
The Place of Resurrection . . . March 18, 1974
The Resurrection and the Life . . . January 1, 1978
The Second Easter . . . March 20, 1978
Stranger on the Road . . . April 2, 1977
Good Friday . . . April 13, 1974
Holy Saturday . . . November 14, 1974
Easter . . . November 11, 1974
Requiem . . . January 24, 1976

IV. The Gifts of God

The Gifts of God . . . February-April, 1978